A Kind of Praying

Rex Chapman

A Kind of Praying

SCM PRESS LTD

334 01253 8

First published 1970
by SCM Press Ltd
56 Bloomsbury Street London WC1

© SCM Press Ltd 1970

Printed in Great Britain by
Northumberland Press Ltd
Gateshead

To Margaret, Doris and Charles

I would like to acknowledge my indebtedness to the many people who either personally or through their writings have influenced these prayers, and especially I thank the Rev. Preb. Tom Baker, whose encouragement was instrumental in preparing the prayers for publication.

Introduction

It is often said that there is a great gulf fixed between the New Testament evidence for the life and teaching of Jesus of Nazareth and the experience of twentieth-century man. The problem is partly the difficulty of the gospel narratives in that they were written for a people living in a culture almost totally alien to our own, and partly our relative, if frequently superficial, familiarity with many of these narratives which thereby lose much of their freshness and challenge.

The meditations in this book are based on the belief that the Christian life develops and grows through a radical juxtaposition of the biblical witness to Jesus and a person's everyday experience of life. Thus we need to let the problems and insights of experience ask critical questions of the Jesus story, and similarly let this story ask questions of our experience. Prayer then becomes more than so much 'babbling on' (NEB Matt. 6.7) and is thoroughly grounded in the facts of life and 'the things concerning Jesus'.

Let it be clearly stated, however, that these reflections are not intended as a simple collection of prayers. Rather they are offered as a way of praying, or more particularly as one man's way of trying to take seriously both the world of the gospels and the experience of life. In short, they are an attempt at praying the Bible.

They are presented in four sections – the parables of Jesus, the Sermon on the Mount, some of the stories about Jesus and the Easter Event – with the aim of covering a wide selection of the teaching of Jesus and many of the stories written about him. Readers are encouraged to use these reflections in so far as they are found helpful, and to let the words and stories about Jesus confront them afresh with the encouragement and challenge of the gospel, and lead them into prayer.

Contents

Some Parables of Jesus

Some of the parables of Jesus are the focus for the reflections in this first section of prayers. Many of the parables as we now read them in the gospels have probably been elaborated and developed by constant use in the worship of the early church. We cannot be sure that the context in which they have been placed by the evangelists was the original one, nor is it always clear that the point they are making in their present position in the gospels is the same point that Jesus made. However, the parables form an important part of the teaching of Jesus and, taking into account what has been said above, we have chosen a selection of them on which to focus our attention.

Old and New

Mark 2.21-22

There is an elderly man who lives nearby.
He often stops me in the street for a chat.
We get on well together, and he talks interestingly of his past.
Yet I can't help thinking, Lord, of the old wineskins.
His views are fixed and allow for no compromise.
There is no room for anything new.
It would take a miracle, a minor revolution, for him to change
  his attitudes to life.

The trouble starts, Lord, when we reach too many conclusions.
The mind is made up.
The matter is closed.
There is nothing more to be said.
The radicalism of the past becomes the conservatism of the
  present.
Keep my mind open to the newness of your gospel.
Keep me always growing to maturity, growing into union with
  you.
Keep me from ever thinking that I am there.

Seed is Sown but not All of It Grows

Mark 4.3-9

I watched the small child, Lord, as he ran to his parents.
He was bubbling with enthusiasm, with joy, with some – for him –
    tremendous piece of news.
His mother was smiling, seeking to share his excitement.
His father looked worried, preoccupied.
He probably only heard the garbled and incoherent remarks.
The one who had ears to hear did hear and shared something of
    what the child was eager to communicate.
The other heard, but did not understand.
Seed falls where it is directed, but not all of it grows.

It is strange, Lord, how different people react in different ways to
    the same situation.
It is strange how I react differently to life at different times.
Sometimes I share the excitement of the child.
I see clearly ahead.
I understand the issues.
I know the way to go.
My eyes are sharply focussed.
The seed grows and bears fruit.
Why can't it be like this always, Lord?
Sometimes I find myself wrestling with an issue, and yet cannot
    see the wood for the trees.
Nothing goes right.
There seems to be nothing I can do.
It is as if the thistles were choking life out of the seed.
Sometimes my interest is aroused.
I begin to get to grips with a job.
Then suddenly the mood changes. Lethargy takes control, and
    enthusiasm becomes a thing of the past.
Interest withers for lack of moisture.
Sometimes I wander wondering what to do.
Life becomes time to be passed.

Nothing stirs any interest.
All seeds have become meals for the birds.

Develop my insight, Lord, into the many different situations in
which I find myself.
Let the seed grow within me and bear fruit.
Let me hear your gospel in the particular moments of my life,
and understand.

As small as a Mustard Seed

Mark 4.30-32

It is good to know this, Lord.
It is good to know that your Kingdom is the end, the goal, the
    purpose of life.
It gives meaning and depth to life.
It makes sense of death.
You stand above the kingdoms of men.
You stand above the kingdom within, where I sit firmly installed
    as king.
It is good to know this, Lord.
My kingdom cannot always bear to let you in.
It is good to know that however small the beginnings, your King-
    dom prevails in the end.
'Amen. Come, Lord Jesus.'

The Critical Moment

Mark 13.33-37

He looked a bit jaded, Lord, as he walked along the gutter.
He might have been fifty years old – or seventy – or anywhere in
    between.
His overcoat had seen better days.
So had his shoes.
He was probably getting a pound or two for his labour.
As he walked past the crowds, he looked as disinterested as they
    in the message displayed front and rear.
'The End Is At Hand.
Prepare To Meet Thy God.'

It is all so unreal, Lord.
The end of what?
Do we not meet already?
For me the crisis is in the present.
You confront me in my neighbour.
You confront me unawares.
You look out from behind the tired eyes of the sandwich-board
    man.
You are having a pint at the bar as I walk into the pub.
You are standing at the doorstep when I answer the door.
You are present, sometimes seen, sometimes hidden, in all my
    relationships.
You jog my memory about an obligation still pending.
You confront my conscience.
You support my life.
The encounter is now. The meeting is today.
If we meet only at the end, Lord, then the end must be now.
Keep me awake to your eternal presence.

'The Lord of the Dance'

Matthew 11.16-19

I feel pressurized, Lord,
Squeezed by the demands that are made of me,
Caught in the crossfire of opinions of what I ought to do, of who
 I ought to be.
One man activates deep feelings, emotions, buried guilt within me.
Another has definite views that hide a latent judgment.
Yet another wants to mould me into his own image.
I feel pressurized into dancing to a multitude of tunes.
It is emotional blackmail, and it is remarkably effective.
My mind is in turmoil.
So many tunes are being piped at once.
For comfort I feel as if I must satisfy them all.
Yet this is impossible.
They are contradictory tunes.
I lack the resources to pay off the blackmail.

John the Baptist lived an ascetic life.
And he, so they said, was as mad as a hatter.
You played it the other way, Lord.
You enjoyed a good meal with your friends – a pity they were
 so unacceptable.
And you, so they said, were a layabout.
It is impossible to win this game, Lord,
                to satisfy all demands, all expectations.
The rules are fixed so that the piper always wins.

'And yet God's wisdom is proved right by its results.'
You are the wisdom of God.
You are the 'Lord of the Dance'.
You withstood the pressures of life to reach the goal of full man-
 hood.
Strengthen me, Lord, when under pressure.
Lead me in the dance.

Inner Resource

Matthew 12.43-45

When a challenge has been successfully fulfilled, Lord,
When a time of quiet and reflection has proved an experience of
　great value,
When some temptation has been defeated,
When I feel my faith deepened, if only a little,
Euphoria encompasses all that I am.
I experience your joy.
I feel strengthened, supported, at peace with the world.
My life takes on a new dimension, previously only glimpsed in
　the distance, now surrounding me, widening my view.
It is as if you are present, with me, closer than a companion at my
　side, too close to be touched.
You are giving yourself to me.
You are within.
The graciousness of yourself is the gift.
It is a vulnerable position to be in, Lord.
All is so well, life is so good, that the slipping back to the old
　ways brings with it an overwhelming wave of disappointment,
　disillusion.
The spirits are back with their friends.
Stay within, Lord, after the joy of encounter has passed.
Remain with me, occupying the house, in my daily life, in the
　normal routine, in my ordinary affairs.
Be an inner resource.

A Mixed Crop

Matthew 13.24-30

It is well-nigh impossible to see what goes on inside a man, Lord.
It is harder than spotting darnel among wheat.
What I see may be as through a glass darkly.
What I see may be influenced by my prejudices.
What I see can only be on the surface.
The inner motives, the hidden life of another man's mind, the
    dark recesses of his personality remain largely unseen to
    outsiders, unseen often to the person himself.
There was that sixteen-year-old boy, submissively polite when
    face to face, gentle with children, a hot-blooded individualist
    who stood out like a wild fire among his friends.
His parents were divorced and dead.
What is going on inside him as he comes to terms with life is
    anybody's guess.
One moment wheat, another moment darnel.
I, along with all, am too eager to label a man, to pigeon-hole him
    for my own security.
In myself, Lord, the wheat grows alongside the darnel.
It is as difficult to judge myself as it is to judge others.
Give me patience.
Give me the sense of proportion to join with all in the human
    endeavour.
Give me the courage to live shoulder to shoulder with the next
    man.
Wheat and darnel grow together in me.
They grow together in him.
Any judgment is yours alone.

Joy in Discovery

Matthew 13.44-46

There is the joy, Lord, of a couple gaining confidence in each
  other as they fall and grow in love.
There is the joy that goes out to welcome the new – the joy of a
  new birth, the joy of discovery, embraced as deepening and
  enriching, not threatening, life.
There is the joy which a man finds in his work and which trans-
  forms the tiring labour of it into delight.
The joy is infectious.
It is seen by all.
But the experience at its source is as hidden to others as the
  treasure in a field.

Your reality, your presence is like this, Lord.
It brings joy, assurance. These urge me to throw everything into
  a life lived in the knowledge that you are on the side of man,
  that joy not sorrow is the response to life that you would
  have a man make.
It urges me to total commitment, even through the lengthy times
  when you remain as hidden to me as you are to many others.
It is the joy of knowing that life is good at its deepest level, no
  matter what may befall a man.

Let me communicate this joy to others, Lord.
Let me stake my life on it.

Forgiveness: the Cross Within

Matthew 18.23-35

You forgive a man his failures, Lord.
I am assured of this.
I accept it with gratitude.
To experience life as worthwhile and joyful and free is to know
    your forgiveness.
This overlaps to others.
It overlaps to the person who comes with apologies, with admis-
    sions of weakness and failure.
It overlaps to the person who makes suitable restitution.
Forgiveness here, Lord, is readily forthcoming.
The debt to my pride is paid.
But there are those who act as if they think me a fool.
There was the insult of that man who thought me stupid enough
    for his confidence trick, and got away with it.
There is the person whose crime is to be so self-confident and
    efficient, so capable and self-assured, so rounded in personality,
    that he reinforces that sense of inferiority.
When pride is hurt, forgiveness flows less easily.
When the deeply ingrained edges of two personalities rub against
    each other, the wounds are tender and take time to heal.
Strengthen my knowledge of your acceptance of me, Lord.
This alone is a basis for confidence sufficient to allow me to see
    straight, sufficient to allow me to forgive those whom I wish
    I did not have to forgive, sufficient to allow me to face the
    cross of forgiveness within.

Talents

Matthew 25.14-29

She lacked confidence in herself, Lord.

She found life hard.

She was afraid to go out of the house by herself.

She was afraid of the world outside the security of her four walls.

She no longer met her son from school.

Her husband did the shopping on his way from work, and took her along every fortnight at first to meet the psychiatrist at his outpatient clinic.

It was strange, Lord, how this woman's world closed in on her.

She had abilities.

She had talents.

She had been a secretary before she married.

Her talents had atrophied.

Even those she had disappeared.

It would not be fair to blame her for her loss of nerve.

But what abilities she had were slowly being lost.

This seems to be true of life, Lord.

One man has a gift of insight. As he uses it, it develops and grows. If he refuses to use it, he becomes as unable to see to the heart of a matter as if he were blind.

Another man has a gift of listening. He can get alongside a person and give confidence and strength as he listens. His talent grows and his wisdom increases. Once he becomes garrulous, the gift is gone.

Yet another has a gift of speaking. He helps men understand the issues in a problem, and with use his gift matures. Let him speak, or he might as well be dumb.

Help me, Lord, to see what talents I have.

Let me not think that I have what I have not, nor that I have not what I have.

Support me as I use them.

Separation is Now

Matthew 25.31-46

There is a wretched side to this story, Lord.
It would seem that even your love is not big enough to embrace
    those who reject your will.
It would seem that even your love has strings attached.
Yet on Golgotha I see you identified with the goats.
On Golgotha I see the depth of your love.

I do not believe, Lord, that you really expect me to love because
    of fear of punishment or hope of reward.
I do not believe that you could look on unmoved as any man was
    consigned to the fire.

I believe that you are confronting me with the urgency to love.
I believe that you are challenging me to see your presence in
    those who suffer.

The separation is now.
I stand on your right hand as you work your will through me.
I stand on your left hand as I sidestep the gospel.
Enable me to see your presence in my neighbour.
Enable me to welcome your presence within me.
You are the source of love and your love reaches out to all.

Despised Neighbour

Luke 10.25-37

Who is my neighbour?
It is just as well that the attacked man in the parable was
    unconscious.
It is hard to accept help from someone I do not get on with very
    well.
But he is my neighbour.
This parable, Lord, must be the most well-known story you told;
Told and retold from primary school days onwards;
Turned into a moral tale;
Edifying;
To be a good samaritan.
The neighbour of the man robbed and unconscious was the
    despised Samaritan.
My neighbour to be loved is the person with whom I find it the
    hardest to make friends.
He is the person I secretly dislike,
The person I want to avoid,
The person with whom I would wish to have no future.
This is no edifying moral tale.
This is to present me with a challenge, to make demands of my
    powers of love, to stretch them to the full.
This is to shake me out of my easy-going charity.
I know myself too well, Lord.
I am afraid that it will not work.
It is an impossible task you set me – impossible in my own
    strength.
Work within me.
Live within me.
Be present within me to revolutionize my love and turn it out-
    wards to the neighbours consciously and unconsciously
    rejected by me.

Rich and Foolish

Luke 12.16-21

Many a person would envy the rich man.
The oriental farmer on the breadline would look at the massive
storehouses, newly built, and yearn, covet, riot for his share.
And who would blame him?
To have an abundance is to have freedom from the basic human
needs.
In areas of endemic famine I am the rich man, Lord, storing up
my wealth.
Many a person would envy the rich man.
Sufficient wealth is essential for all men.
Help me, Lord, to give of my resources.

Yet I envy the rich man too some of the time.
Riches are relative to regions, and this is a wealthy region.
What is an abundance in one area is average here.
I look at the storehouses, newly built, and half wish they were
mine.
What good a man could do!
How much freedom he would have!
What possibilities would be opened!
If only, if only the wealth were mine.
Yet deep down I know that, given a sufficiency, life of any
quality is something that is beyond riches.
Deep down I know that whatever goods I possess only whet the
appetite for more.
The other man's grass is always greener.
Life cannot be packed into barns, hoarded against perpetual rainy
days.
The life you give a man is the real wealth, Lord.
It is the wealth of meaning, of hope, of joy, the wealth of faith,
of affirmation, of love, the wealth of life eternal for which a
man might even be prepared to die.
Bring me near to this man, Lord, near to yourself.

One Last Chance

Luke 13.6-9

One last chance you were saying to Israel, Lord.
Is it to be one last chance too for the church?
Your love is strong enough to bear failure.
You lean over backwards to give the fig tree another chance.
 There was life there still, though fruit was lacking.
The 'scandal' of our church, your church, Lord, of us, is com-
 placency, contentment with the way things are when you are
 on the move in the world.
You are the adult man, the man who has realized in himself the
 human potential.
You are on the move throughout the world to make men human.
The 'glory' of our church, your church, is when it allows you
 freedom of movement within it; when it lets you reveal in
 your Body, in us, in me, the reflection of your humanity.

How long will your patience last, Lord, with the church, with us,
 with me?
How long before this church is discarded as a hindrance to your
 mission in the world?

Work within me, within us, within the church.
Be at the centre of our lives.
Mould us in your image.
Bring about our transformation.
Make us fruitful, Lord,
Now,
Here as well as there,
Me as well as others.

Front Seat, Back Seat

Luke 14.7-11

Status.
Academic hoods, Lord?
Reserved seats?
Jockeying for position?
Those letters after a man's name?
Some Christians more reverend than others?
Titles?
To want to be seen to be somebody is the real inferiority complex.
It reveals the shifting source of our search for salvation.
It reveals that we are still young on the road to maturity.
Enable me to be myself, without side, without pretence.
Strengthen my knowledge that I am accepted by you, Lord.
This is the only ultimate status that I know.

But there is more subtle play still, Lord, especially potent because
    it seems to be in keeping with the style of the parable.
Playing down accomplishments, the forced humility, taking the
    back seat deliberately so as to be seen to be brought to the
    front.
Then are not respect and status doubly sure?
Enable me to put the other man first, Lord.
Strengthen my knowledge that I am accepted by you.
This is the only ultimate status that I know.

It is One Big Party

Luke 14.16-24

Your Kingdom, Lord, is here and now.
It is in this place, at this moment in time, with these people.
You are calling men together, to your feast.
You stand waiting, a focus among men, the centre around whom
    we are to converge.
You are at the core of community.
You are at the heart of shalom.
You are at the meeting-point of reconciliation.
Your feast is laid ready – the universal Eucharist.
Mankind is invited.
We are the guests.

I urgently want mankind to be united, the world to be one.
The invitation to drop in for the party is easily accepted for
    there and then, in another place, at some other time, with
    unspecified people.
I can demonstrate and shout for a future Utopia with the best
    of them.
But it is here and now, in this place, at this time, in this situation,
    with these people that your Kingdom is to be found.
Ground my faith in this fact, Lord.
It is with the friendly, the amusing, the hostile, the compassionate,
    the anxious, the joyful, the angry, the grief-ridden, the insin-
    cere, the tearful, the unlovable, the honest men, women and
    children with whom I meet today that your Kingdom is to be
    found.
Press home your invitation, Lord.
Widen my horizons.
Enable me to see your presence speaking through the people I
    meet.
Before it is too late.
Before tomorrow comes.

Building a Tower or Castles in the Air?

Luke 14.27-33

You pull no punches, Lord.
Your gospel is not cheap, to be had in the bargain basement, at
    cut rates.
I sometimes wish it were.
That fine old building, a summer's evening, the sound of bells
    floating across the meadows, the choir singing an anthem, a
    few well-chosen words – all beautiful, charming, edifying and
    designed to send me to sleep.
No problems here; no cross to be seen.
A delightful service, a pleasant experience away from the ten-
    sions of life.

You would have me believe that to be a Christian is a much more
    worldly business, Lord,
Preparations, calculations, assessments to be made within the
    normal run of life.
Are the implications clear? – they are only too clear.
Are your demands reasonable? – they are excessive for a man on
    his own.
Can I stand the pace? – it remains to be seen.

Lord, lead me to your activity in the world.
Lead me along the Via Dolorosa, the way of the cross.
But I need your support to bear the weight of the cross I have to
    shoulder.
You carried yours.
This encourages me to take the plunge again and again.
Sometimes I fail, like the man with the foundations laid, but left
    unfinished like a ruin.
Sometimes you succeed through me; you finish the job.
I am yours, Lord.
Make me yours.

A Sheep and a Coin: Lost and Found

Luke 15.1-10

A sheep is such a stupid creature, Lord.
It is the original conformist.
It is synonymous with the herd instinct of crowds – or the Sunday lunch.

And a coin – a coin is a useful thing, but a thing nonetheless.
It has no value in itself.
It is symbolic of one level of interchange between people.

I feel like neither a sheep nor a coin, Lord.
They can never be other than they are.
Neither can repent.
But it is good to know this, Lord. It shows that your mercy has no strings attached.
You take the initiative.
You seek a man out, as a shepherd seeks a sheep,
                         as a woman looks for her coin.
You seek me out.
Sometimes I am too swift for you.
I run hell-for-leather along my own self-righteous road, the road on which I justify myself by my actions.
Sometimes, thank God, I am caught.
And capture is repentance.
Then your joy 'among the angels of God' is contagious.
It lifts me out of myself to share in this joy.

'Lord Jesus Christ, Son of God, have mercy on me, a sinner.'

Two Lost Sons

Luke 15.11-32

Jealousy is a powerful force, Lord.

It springs up within at the success or the nerve or the ability of someone close.

That man over there is free to act as he wishes; no ties bind us together.

This man here, Lord, is a different matter.

I know him well.

I am too close to be free from the problems this brings.

I sympathize with the elder brother.

No doubt he was jealous of his brother taking the initative in the way he did. After all he *was* the elder brother.

And then when he had the chance to say 'I told you so!', what happens? – a lavish welcome from his father after all his younger son had done.

I too would have felt mad, Lord.

I too would have felt indignant.

I too need your deliverance from the jealousy that sours a relationship.

I too need the breadth of vision that life brought to the younger son.

I need your freedom.

It is not always easy to say this, Lord.

Occasionally I can when life is at a low ebb, or when I look inside and do not like what I see.

Usually I prefer the superficial freedom that keeps me happy, and stops me looking too deep.

Break in, Lord.

Let your 'wind of change' sweep through me.

You hold nothing against a man.

The Unjust Judge and the Ideal Man

Luke 18.1-8

If even an unjust judge gives way to persistence in a cause that is
 right, how much more readily will you listen, Lord, to a man's
 just desire.

Built into every man is an ideal man.
He may not know it, he may not think much about it, but it is
 there as the standard against which the real is measured.
It is seen in a man's ambitions, in his actions, in his dreams.
The ideal man is the sort of person the flesh and blood man wants
 to be, or even feels he is.
He is the guide who motivates action, the image who drives
 ambition, the myth who moulds behaviour.
The ideal man is the shadow image with whom we try to merge.
That adolescent boy, Lord, has a vision of competence, greatness
 in sport, and works hard at imitation.
That young man is eager to reach the top of the business world.
This woman strives to fulfil her motherhood.
This man is a thinker. His ideal man, spurring him on from the
 depths of his soul, is the free and independent and profound
 commentator on life.

Lord, all these people persist in their pursuit of the ideal man
 within, and seek to turn him into reality.
The ideal man within me has been created by the influences of
 many people, many events.
Fashion him in your image, the image of the new man, the real
 Adam.
Grant me strength to persist in reflection, meditation, prayer on
 the nature of who man is, who I am, what he ought to be like,
 what I ought to be like.
Let me persist in faith in you.
Be with me, be within me fashioning my being into conformity
 with you.

The Sermon on the Mount

The focus of the following prayers and reflections is the Sermon on the Mount. Matthew has collected into the Sermon that material which he regarded as the core of the teaching of Jesus, and he has presented it in such a way that it can be seen to supersede the Law of the Old Testament. Modern scholarship has made it clear that Jesus as a historical personality did not 'preach' the Sermon as we now have it, because his words and deeds seem to have been remembered and preserved in separate units collected together later by the evangelists. Nevertheless Matthew believed that he was putting before his readers the heart of the gospel, and it is this 'heart of the gospel' which forms the basis for the reflective prayers which follow.

How Poor is Poor?

Matthew 5.1-3

How well they sound, Lord, those 'beatitudes', but bring them
    home to me.

How blest are those who know that they are poor
My poverty is a limited poverty.
Money may be short at times, but it is there.
And I have the talents, the abilities, you gave me.
Am I not investing them wisely in my education, my life, my
    activities?
My poverty is a limited poverty.

Bring me to see that what I have is there to be shared.
Bring me to see that what I have is not the last word in life.
Bring me to see that ultimately my security, my peace of mind
    depends not on my talents,
            not on my achievements,
            not on the status that goes with these,
            but on knowing that all that I have
    gains its meaning from you.
To know this, Lord, is to know both poverty and riches.

Regrets

Matthew 5.4

How blest are the sorrowful
Why did I have to say it?
There was really no need.
It was a superfluous comment, spoken without thinking.
He was obviously hurt – and to no purpose.
Why did I have to say it?

Regrets, Lord, make the past exceedingly real to the present.
They force a man to relive what is past.
They make it that bit harder to live the present.
This comment,
That action,
Those omissions;
It can never be as if they had never been.

My regrets, Lord, are many;
Regrets that what I am is less than it might be;
Regrets too, sometimes, that the easy peace, the easy security,
    the apathy that engulfs so much of what I am is at its heart
    unsatisfying;
Regrets from which you alone can take the sting.
You alone can enable us to live with ourselves for the future in
    your strength.

The Spirit of Life or Death?

Matthew 5.5

How blest are those of a gentle spirit
It is that deadening inertia, Lord, 'gravity', the meekness that is
    really fear.
This is what I try to pretend is what you want.
But I know that it is not.
It is an anxious cowardice that keeps me quiet when I ought to
    speak.
It is fear of a scene that produces platitudes instead of truth.
It is an over-eagerness to keep everybody happy that hinders the
    working of your Spirit.
It is the spirit of death that holds me back from grappling with
    life.
Take away, Lord, this mockery.
Put in its place the gentleness of spirit defined by your life –
The spirit that strives for the truth,
            that endures with patience,
            that holds its peace when reproached,
            that holds self back for the sake of another,
            that uses constructively the emotions that well up
                inside,
The gentleness of spirit not based on fear,
                    but on the knowledge that in spite of
    myself I am an instrument of your challenging love.

Sometimes I Do

Matthew 5.6

How blest are those who hunger and thirst to see right prevail
Sometimes I do, but God it is hard.
You seem to ask too much.
Not knowing what it is to be really hungry and really thirsty,
    only in imagination can I begin to know the extent of what
    you ask.
Shake me out of my indifference.
Shake me out of my satisfaction with partial righteousness.
Shake me until I see the need for right to prevail wherever life
    exists.
But most important, Lord: Let me not flee from my responsibilities
    here where I can do something,
    by turning my mind many miles away where I can do little.
Bring me to work for right to prevail in those areas of life in
    which I move and where I can be involved.

Small Change or All I Have?

Matthew 5.7

How blest are those who show mercy
How glib it all sounds.
As glib as the words of Portia, 'The quality of mercy is not
    strained, it droppeth as the gentle rain from heaven.'
To show mercy is not easy.

Ten new pence to the man who calls at the door to assuage cons-
    cience and remove the problem.
Sitting on a few of the relevant committees.
This is relatively easy, Lord.
All that is lost is a bit of time, a bit of leisure, and some small
    change.

It is not easy to give something of myself,
                to work hard for few clearly-seen results,
                to stay around where the need is great and bear
    the pain of feeling a failure,
                to be involved deeply and fully in human suffering.
To show mercy is not easy.

Give me the insight, Lord, to feel as others feel.
Give me the imagination to stand in another's shoes.
Your mercy is great because you know in Jesus what it is to be
    a man.
Help me to share in this mercy.

'You have Searched Me and Known Me'

Matthew 5.8

How blest are those whose hearts are pure
I look into myself, Lord.
I examine my motives.
I wish to see myself as you see me.
    Do I serve for self-display?
    Is it my own prestige that is uppermost in my mind?
    What stands at the back of this action, that feeling?
My motives, I expect, are mixed.
It is dark inside,
In the depths of my being,
At the core of who I am.
'You have searched me and known me.'
You know, Lord.
You work within.
You seek to mould me in the mind of Christ.

Strengthen my personality.
Enlighten my inner search.
Prevent the self-centredness of excessive scrupulousness.
Point me back to life.

Peace at a Price

Matthew 5.9-12

How blest are the peacemakers . . . and those who suffer persecu-
tion
I find it hard to bring peace where there is no peace.
It is demanding.
Back at home,
Among friends,
With relatives,
It is nice and cosy and comfortable.
In the world,
Among those where the barriers come up,
With those I do not like,
It is far from nice and cosy and comfortable.
Why do I have to love?
Why have I chosen to be a follower of one who loved to the
    utmost?

Strengthen me, Lord, to face the task, the crucifying task, of
    being a reconciler amongst guilt and fear, anxiety and anger.

Bring me, Lord, further to the point where I can accept life with
    all its problems and pains 'with gladness and exultation',
Not because of future perks in a future heaven,
But because I know that to be fully a man, to be fully human,
    I can do no other.

Salt

Matthew 5.13

'You are salt to the world.'
How common it sounds!
Though without it life would be immeasurably reduced.
You are calling me, Lord, to a mission of great consequence.
Salt preserves and sustains and enhances.
It brings out the flavour of a thing.
You are urging me to join with your followers in bringing to
    perfection the full flavour of the universe in which we live.

Prevent me, Lord, from 'becoming tasteless', from turning my
    faith into an individual, pietistic affair, a matter only between
    the two of us.
Throw me into the world, into the society in which I am living,
    to help bring out its true nature.

And yet partly I am afraid.
It is a precipitous course, the risks are incalculable.
You were 'edged out of the world and on to the cross'.
The same might happen to a man who takes you too seriously.
And partly I cannot summon up the enthusiasm to bother, to
    change my ways, to break out of the rut, to be different.
    It is an effort.
Sometimes I seem to be saying – it is good to be a Christian, but
    not too Christian.
'But if the salt becomes tasteless . . .'

The Glare of a City at Night

Matthew 5.14-16

Light is seen.
It guides.
It cannot be missed.
It does not hide itself in corners, but probes them out.
You are making me a marked man, Lord, a focus, clearly to be
seen like the phosphorescent glare of a city at night.
Are you making me a Pharisee, Lord, the pious man who stands
at the altar beating his breast and proclaiming like a prophet
of doom the sins of the world?
Is this what you want me to be?
A man shouting from the rooftops – I am saved brother, what
about you?
Brother sees only the glare, blinded to the gospel.

No, Lord, this is not your meaning.
'Shed light among your fellows that they may give praise to your
Father in heaven.'
You are the 'light of the world' calling me to you,
calling me to reflect your reality
and your presence among all your people.

I am not worthy, Lord.
The nearer I come to you, the greater the gulf between us.
You are all that I am not.
You forgive those who tie you to the cross.
Was it a struggle for you? It is for me.
You reveal the graciousness and compassion that is at the heart
of our universe.
Draw me to you, the 'real light which enlightens every man'.
In this is hope.
Not in my own efforts to shine like a beacon,
But to be the channel for your light to shine through all my
activities, all the areas of my interests, all my plans and hopes
and motives, to shine throughout the whole of my life.

The Right Side of the Law

Matthew 5.17-20

Thank God Matthew extols the law.
I know where I am when the rules are down in black and white.
I can get my life taped, organized, neatly parcelled and packed.
I know what I can do and what I cannot.
It is so much easier, Lord, that I hardly have to think for myself.
Let the church lay down the rules, the way of salvation, then all
    I need is the strength to follow.
I wish it were so simple!

There is more to it still, Lord.
The law has formed my character – the law of conventional rules,
    the law of moral values, of cultural norms, of religious ideals,
    of educational possibilities – the law of all the forces which
    have formed me into the person I am.
With Matthew I can give thanks for this law.
It is 'holy and just and good'.

But didn't you, Lord, incur the wrath of the authorities by break-
    ing the law, by healing on the Sabbath, by turning conventions
    upside down?
You went beyond conventional rules, conventional law, to the
    Law of God.
You brought law to completion.
You brought out its real meaning.
You saw it as the ground, the necessary ground, but only the
    ground, out of which transformation springs.

Guide me, Lord, to look to the basis of my faith, not to be satisfied
    with half-truths;
With a life that is 'partly living' and a love that is partly loving.
Guide me to give thanks for my personal past, my tradition, that
    has made me what I am.
But take me beyond this: bring about my transformation.
This means:
Bring me to see that my desires to be self-sufficient are insufficient.
It is satisfying to feel that I can do your will of my own freewill.

I haven't the humility to admit to dependence in days when independence is so great an ideal.

Enable me, Lord, to put your flesh on the bones of independence.

You entrusted yourself to God and became the most independent of men, with the freedom to live as a man in the image of God.

Enable me, Lord, to be a 'better man than the Pharisees and doctors of the law',

not because I become a stricter adherent than they to rules, however religious they might be,

not because I am satisfied with myself and my past, but because

I want a future, a life transformed and lived in you, among men.

Anger is Murder

Matthew 5.21-22

You press the point to the ultimate degree.
It is impossible, Lord, in the world as it is not 'to nurse anger
    against a brother'.
Is this the point?
If we all stand guilty,
If we all 'must be brought to judgment',
If we all experience the 'hell' of regret,
There can be no separating sheep from goats.

I, along with all, am in need of your grace.

Lord, Where are You?

Matthew 5.23-24

Lord, where are you?
It is like talking to thin air, a will 'o the wisp projection, that
    comes and goes.
Are you myth or real?
God knows.

The altar is real.
The Eucharist is real.
There I am met, encountered.
There is peace, the challenging peace that bounces me back, like
    a springboard, into life, bounces me back renewed, strength-
    ened, bound firmly into the Body of Christ.

That grievance with a brother.
It needles me.
It is at the back of my mind, eating away at my joy.
It will not go away.
No peace now at the altar.
Only judgment.

Drive me to my knees, Lord.
Drive me to conquer my pride.
Drive me to my brother, Lord.
Drive me to the reconciliation without which the eucharist, the
    thanksgiving, becomes an empty shell.

Sued

Matthew 5.25-26

You make it sound like expediency.
You make it sound as if fear of consequences ought to be my
    guide.
Perhaps I take you too literally.

A relationship founders,
A marriage is on the rocks,
A family on the streets,
A man out of a job,
A woman has a miscarriage,
Life goes on as it always has.

Let me not pass by on the other side.
Let me not stand before you as the defendant sued for being want-
    ing in concern.
To pass by on the other side is slowly to build the bars of my
    prison until it is escapeproof.
Then it becomes home.
Is this the way it will be, Lord – with me?
Deliver me from myself.
Involve me in life.
Involve yourself with me, Lord.

Those Fantasies

Matthew 5.27-32

You will turn us all into adulterers, Lord!
Thoughts, ideas, pictures flood into my mind.
The more barricades I put up, the greater the force against them.
There is nothing so perverse as the way these fantasies fill my
    thoughts.
The more I will not to receive them, the more they attack.

What is that you say?
I try too hard?
I worry too much about myself?
I need to turn outwards to the world?

Then strengthen me for this, Lord.
Enable me to appreciate the beauty of a woman without it turning
    me inwards upon myself.
Give me the wisdom to understand the real world of the joys and
    tensions, pleasures and pains of intimate relationships, of mar-
    riage and divorce.
'Tear out and fling aside' my fantasy world.
Lead me into your world, the real world.

There was One Man who Stood like a Fish out of Water . . .

Matthew 5.33-37

There were only about twelve of us in court, Lord.
The man I had come with stood in the dock like a fish out of water.
Shabbily dressed, an epileptic, with a tongue that could not always
   be trusted, a regular communicant at your eucharist.
He had been provoked, and had hit out.
I was in the witness box called to try and help the court decide
   what would be the best for him.
I was asked to swear an oath on the Bible.
Did they think I was going to lie?
It was a meaningless charade, Lord.
What I had to say, I would say.
In court, it seems, oaths are sworn as witness to the lack of truth.
Make me transparent to your truth, Lord.
Make it needless for me to justify myself with or without an oath.

. . . and Another who Swore like a Trooper

But times have changed.
There was that man in uniform. He swore like a trooper.
He called on you, Lord, many times.
Perhaps you heard him.
He spent much of his free time making entertainment for the
   patients, your people, in a hospital for the subnormal.
His swearing seemed irrelevant.
He was doing your will.
He loved.
Perhaps too his swearing was your fault, Lord.
His son was a mongol.
He was saying by his action a plain 'yes' to life and 'no' to despair,
   self-pity.

Deepen my faith, Lord.
Enable me to live and speak the truth.

Who can Love so much?

Matthew 5.38-48

Do not set yourself against the man who wrongs you
Here is the crunch.
My love is too small.
I was ignored at that party.
I was snubbed by an acquaintance.
I was insulted not to have been invited.
My work was not appreciated.
I was made to feel small.
Resentment rose within me. I wanted to hit back, to retaliate.
One cheek was quite enough.

I know my rights; sometimes I stand on them.
I can be expected to allot one hour for this man's need, but the
    rest of the evening is my own.
He can have the shirt, but it is hard to part with the coat.

My duty has definite limits.
I will go with him a mile, but I find plenty of excuses to save me
    going two.

Small change for Christian Aid.
I need the rest for that snack between meals, that night at the
    cinema.

Your call, Lord, has no limits.
You set no bounds.
On my own it is impossible; it is beyond my powers.
Help.

Love your enemies
From bad to worse.
Are you mad, Lord?
Do you expect me to follow on these terms?
Now if you relaxed them just a little . . .
But no.
You died rather than fail your vision of love.

53

You leave me no choice.
You force me to my knees.
You force me to turn to you.
Your demands seek to revolutionize my life.
I submit.
But it will be a long haul.
Bring me to the point where I can say – Father, forgive them.

The Big Show

Matthew 6.1-6, 16-18

What the motive is – that is the point.
There is a woman down the road.
She is a widow.
She calls to see a near-blind neighbour, living alone, most days of
the week.
I know her well, Lord, but I have only just learned of this – in
passing.
She gains little in 'admiration from men'.
I do not think that she does it for any reward 'in your Father's
house in heaven'.
She does it because she is a caring person.
Her reward might be an inner satisfaction, a sense that she is
doing your will.
Her love goes outside herself to a person with a need.

I feel judged, Lord.
You see I seem to be different.
I like that 'flourish of trumpets'.
It boosts my ego – to be seen to be doing your will.
Do I hear you say that it is not your will?
In the depths of my soul I know that this is true.
Work through me, Lord, so that your will, not mine, *is* done.

Again, when you pray . . .
This is different, Lord.
I am not so keen to be seen praying as I am doing acts of charity.
I am more likely to be thought odd than saintly.
It is all right when there are some of us together. We support each
other, especially in church.
It is expected that people in churches pray.
On my own I am only too keen, when I pray at all, to 'go into a
room by myself and shut the door'.
What I need is the courage to follow you, Lord, into the desert;
                              to allow my complacency to be
shattered again and again;
                              to enable you to break through the
images I have of myself, so that I can see myself as I am.

What I need is the spirit of openness to whatever you have in
   store for me.
Throughout this, Lord, I need your sustaining love.
This is reward.
Enable me to face all this in the midst of life, in the midst of your
   world.

So too when you fast . . .
How seriously he takes his religion!
He fasts, he goes to church, he is on lots of committees.
Anyone can see what a fine person he is.

Is this the image I want others to have of me, Lord?
Are the things I do, done openly for applause?
Worse, am I doing them 'in secret' to gain your approval?
Perhaps you know. I do not.
Motives are complex, bound together like the strands in a rope.

One thing I ask:
Please make me more the person who lives out his faith
   with sincerity,
   with honesty,
   without humbug.

'Do not Go Babbling On'

Matthew 6.7-15

Silence before you, Lord.
Waiting,
Listening,
Before speaking . . .

This prayer, your prayer, I know so well, too well.
It slips by, spoken so often.

Our Father in heaven
Frequently I wonder.
A spastic child,
A woman blind from birth,
A husband and father killed by thrombosis in the prime of life.
Pain and suffering.
I wonder, Lord.
Why should it be so?
I know no answer.
I only know that you suffered too.

In this world, the real earthy world where much is less than ideal,
    you urge me to say 'yes' to life, to say 'Father', to affirm that
    there is meaning and hope and love and compassion at the
    heart of things.
Bring me to this faith, Lord.
Strengthen me in this faith.
But force me too to face the many harsh realities of life, even those
    that cast their shadow over me – those that I wish I could
    avoid.
Deepen my faith in you, in spite of . . .

Your Kingdom come, your will be done
This is a prayer for revolution, a constant overthrowing of values,
    a call for all men to respond in life-long commitment to you,
    Lord, and to your activity in the world.
It is tempting to despair of it happening.

As Jesus of Nazareth you focussed the Kingdom in your life.
But the world had no place for you.
You were too revolutionary.
You touched people where it hurt.
You spoke parables with a sting in the tail.
You called men to total commitment.
Even your closest friends ran for cover.
You were so uncompromising.
So that was that.
For three days.

Now you are alive as Lord, vindicated.
You reign wherever men acknowledge in their lives your gospel
    of reconciliation.
You reign in the healing work of mankind.
You reign wherever the dividing walls of hostility are broken down,
            wherever men come together in trust and confidence –
    in the settling of an industrial dispute,
    in the concern of the Samaritans,
    in the work of a hospital,
    in families and schools,
    in universities and colleges . . .
Wherever men are,
Wherever they meet together,
You are there.
This is the ground of my confidence, Lord.
This is the foundation for my future.
This is the basis for my prayer – your Kingdom come, your will
    be done.

Give us today our daily bread
The whole of creation depends on you, Lord.
But why so little rain in one part of the world, and more than
    enough in another?
Why famine in one country, while surplus corn can be destroyed
    in another?

Enable men, Lord, to see the world as a unity.
Enable us to pool our resources, to share what we have.

And make it impossible for me to use this prayer without thought
and action for those who have no bread.

Forgive us the wrong we have done, as we forgive . . .
I have plenty of excuses, Lord, that I can produce at the drop
of a hat.
Sometimes they convince others – a pity that they do not convince
me.

Here is one:
I cannot be held responsible for all the wrong I do.
It is my upbringing, my parents' fault, not mine, someone else's
bad influence.
Sometimes consciously, more often unconsciously, have not they
shaped my personality so that I cannot be other than I am?
See that man over there, that man in prison, inadequate, unable to
cope with his job, with his marriage; he drifted into petty
larceny.
Was it really his fault?
He did not ask to be born into a substandard house.
He did not ask his father to fornicate and forget.
He did not ask his mother to fail in parenthood on her own.
Of course I have been luckier in life, in my background.
But is not the argument the same?
I cannot be responsible for all that I am, when I became what
I am before being able to take responsibility.
It seems a good argument, Lord.
I wish it convinced me.
But I know that I am responsible.
I feel responsible.
Not to take responsibility is not to be a man.

It is good to know that I am not on my own.
It is we who are to be forgiven, not simply I.
Forgive us, forgive me, Lord, all that is less that it might have
been, all failures in living.
Remove the guilt that inhibits life and action.
Your forgiveness revitalizes a man.
It frees him from his past, frees him to live and love, to be human
for the future.
It restores his hope.

How can I experience this, Lord, if I do not do the same for my
neighbour?

Do not bring us to the test, but save us . . .
I fear for myself.
I am apprehensive of my strength to cope with a crisis.
I see you, Lord, struggling in the wilderness to work out your
vocation in life, and what it means to live as a man.
I see you wrestling with yourself in Gethsemane.

Take this cup from me, Lord.
I decide for you in my mind, with my intellect,
But the emotional forces within me are powerful; they prefer to
pull me away from the test, to take the easier course, to seek
a false security.

Writings that appeal to baser instincts.
Thoughts that stir my pride.
Actions that are not worthy of a man.
They come naturally.

Give me the sense of proportion, the sense of humour to laugh
them out of their power over me.
Grant me a share in your victory in the wilderness.

My work, my calling in life, what you would have me do in the
moments of decision—
Give me a sense of your vision, the power to act upon it, a share
in your victory in Gethsemane, the remembrance that you are
with me always.

Things

Matthew 6.19-24

I remember a story, Lord, from the early days of the church,
　　during the Decian persecution in Rome.
The authorities burst into the church to loot its treasures.
Laurentius, a deacon, pointed to widows and orphans being cared
　　for, the sick being nursed, the poor having their needs supplied.
These are the treasures of the church.

Things are good in themselves, Lord.
They are part of creation.
How would we live without them?
The ambulance that drives the sick to hospital.
The bus that takes men to work.
The pan that cooks our food.
The clothes that keep us warm.
The books that help us learn.

Things have beauty too, Lord.
Life would be less without enjoyment of it.
The shimmering beauty of finely cut glass.
The aesthetic design of a piece of furniture.
The elegant cut of a dress.
The consummate skill of a sculpture.
The melody of a musical instrument.

The eye that is unsound sees only part of the truth.
It looks through a filter as opaque as a cataract.
It looks at life and distorts what it sees.
It sees a welter of things and is eager to make them possessions.
It competes with the hoarding church – hiding away those silver
　　and jewelled sets of sacrament vessels, never used, never seen,
　　never removed from their dusty corner in some ecclesiastical
　　safe.

Enable me, Lord, to enjoy the usefulness and beauty of things.
Prevent me investing in them my all,
　　　　　　hoarding them and turning them into my idol, my god.
Lead me to invest my all in the treasures of Laurentius.
Lead me to use things in your service, and not in my own.

'Begone, Dull Care; I Prithee, Begone from Me!'

Matthew 6.25-34

I find it paradoxical, Lord, that this fine poetic passage urging the
    casting aside of worry for the future once in fact brought on
    worry.
That insurance policy on my life;
Those savings that mature many years from now;
Those plans for a coming holiday;
That schedule of work;
Am I not expected to think beyond today?

This cannot be, Lord.
When no provision is made for the future, today's anxiety is the
    more.
Charity to my family demands a cool look at the one definite
    certainty of the future – my death.

Do I hear you say that this is in accord with your will?
What you are talking about is not such foresight for the future,
    but the worry about the future that eats away at a man's peace.
Worry about status, about position in life, about wealth,
Unnecessary worry about what other people think,
The everyday worries that inhibit all action today.
Let each day's troubles be sufficient.
'Set your mind on God's Kingdom before anything else.'

The one thing, Lord, that calms my worries, my anxious fears
    is not the accumulation of possessions, though this is tempting;
    it is not even the reassurance of friends, though this is of
    considerable help;
    it is faith and hope – the hope that springs from knowledge of
    your faithfulness to man.
If you are with us, who and what can prevail against us?

Set me free, Lord, from faith and hope in lesser things.
Set me free from commitment to my own blueprints for my own
    future.

Set me free for faith and hope in you.
Set me free for commitment to your plans for my future.

Set me free to live and work and serve building your future.
Set me free, Lord, to be a man.

Who Shall Judge?

Matthew 7.1-12

Judgment is such a final thing, Lord.
It marks an end.
There is nothing more to be said.
The conclusion is reached.
The final assessment is made.

Make me take care about judging, Lord, care not to turn provi-
sional assessments into final judgments.
You yourself stand as witness to the danger of judgment.
You were judged wanting by the authorities.
You were judged unworthy of life.
Judgment destroyed you.

Judgment is destructive too for the man who does the judging.
The 'great plank' destroys the eye so that it can see clearly no more.

He is hard to understand, Lord – that man across the road.
His judgments weigh heavy on his wife and children, and heavier
still on himself.
The chip on his shoulder is isolating him from the joy of human
contact.
It makes people wary of approach.
And this adds fuel to the fire of his judgments, his condemnation
of all around him.
He lives at the centre of a vicious circle, Lord.
As a man judges others, so he himself is judged.

My judgments, Lord, are attempts sometimes to hide my own
faults by pointing to another's.
Sometimes they are attempts to stake out my own claim to sanc-
tity, purity, to the kudos of doing your will, over against the
others who fail.

My judgments are the trampling under foot of your precious gift
of forgiveness and love.
They make me as heavy-footed as those pigs who ignore pearls
for the swill.

64

You compel me to admit this, Lord, uncomfortable though it is.
Draw me away from the hardness of judging.
Lead me into repentance of my own sin, and into charity towards
     others.

These insights of yours, Lord, are not easy to bear.
I need your support.
For this I ask as a son asking for bread.
You are faithful and sure.
You do not mock a man by throwing down a stone.

Small and Narrow

Matthew 7.13-14

A child, waiting to be born, enters the world by the narrow gate.
There is no space to spare.
The passage is tailor-made.
It is an experience that destroys the sleepy security of former
  things.
It is a lonely journey that a man must make on his own.

Is it like this, Lord – the new life lived in you?
                    – a glorious thing that springs from effort,
  labour, a sense of direction?

Yet there is an inevitability about birth, a process once started
  that cannot easily be stopped.
There is no inevitability about the decisions I make, Lord;
                    about the quality of my life;
                    about the strength of my desire to seek
  that narrow gate, as elusive as a mirage in the desert.
I think I am there.
I have it all worked out.
Your calling is clear.
What you would have me do is distinct.
When I arrive the goal is still further ahead.
There is more to be done.
Another stage to go.
Further gated lanes to find.

Perhaps this is as well, Lord – not to see too far into the future.
It is only in looking back that I see the direction in which I am
  going.

Guide me now,
At this moment in time,
In the particular affairs that need to be my present concern,
To follow you who are the Way.

'By their Fruits . . .'

Matthew 7.15-23

He has a charming smile, Lord.
He is forceful.
He knows what he thinks.
He knows where he wants to go.
He is convinced that he knows your will.
He is compelling. He compels me to listen by the strength of his
    personality.
His passion terrifies me.
He is a hard-bitten salesman seeking to sell his wares.
These wares he calls the gospel.

I see writ large in him, Lord, my own and everyman's intolerance.
His 'gospel' latches on to the worst in a man, and rages against
    reconciliation.
Is this why he seems compelling?

Lord, forgive him and me.
Your presence in a man is recognized in actions and attitudes,
    not in pseudo-prayers,
    not in a pseudo-faith that covers life like a veneer,
    not even in sincerely-held, but evil, views.
Use him and me in the service of reconciliation.

The Sand and the Rock

Matthew 7.24-29

I am at the end of the Sermon, Lord.
It is a fine ethic.
I am trying hard to live it.
The trouble is that I have heard it all before.
Its cutting edge is blunted after all these years.
And in any case I cannot always bear to hear what is radically
    new.

It is not so much that I consciously avoid living out your ethic.
It is not even so much that I frequently fail.
It is more subtle than that.
I feel the shifting sand beneath me when your demands simply
    make me want to try harder, as if I can fulfil these demands
    on my own.
No doubt, Lord, you want me to strengthen my will, but I get the
    impression that your demands, your well-nigh impossible de-
    mands, are meant to force me to the floor, to force me to
    admit to my total dependence on you – the rock.

You pick up the pieces of failure.
You stand a man on his feet again.
You stand me on my feet again.
You are the rock sustaining me when the chips are down,
                    sustaining me in crisis.
You urge me to believe that I am not on my own,
                    that I am accepted in spite of myself
    and my inabilities, in spite of my sin, in spite of the fact that
    all my actions and attitudes are less than what you would wish.
You also urge me to believe that yours is the presence sustaining
    my strengths, my abilities, my talents,
                    that you are the rock upon which
    all the positive forces in my life are built.

This is your gospel, Lord.
No wonder people felt that you spoke with authority.
You were speaking good news.

Your demands are colossal, far-reaching.
But I am not on my own.
I am not unforgiven.
I am not left to flounder.
Your demands are infinite. Your support is infinite.
Thank God.

Some Stories about Jesus

With this section of the meditations we move from the teaching of Jesus to some accounts of the events in which he featured. A number of miracle stories together with a few other narratives have been chosen in the belief that the gospel within them has a profound relevance for our contemporary experience of life. In many ways, however, the historicity of these stories causes problems for the Christian of today, and we would recommend the use of a modern commentary as a preliminary to this type of reflective prayer. Indeed, it cannot be stated too strongly that a serious attempt to pray the bible needs to be prefaced by a consideration of the nature of the particular material which is to be used. A brief selection of books for this purpose will, therefore, be found in the appendix.

'The Word Became Flesh'

Matthew 2.1-12; Luke 2.1-20; John 1.1-14

The children were keen, once again, to act the Christmas story.
They kept asking as Christmas drew near.
Can I be Joseph?
Can I be Mary?
Can I be Herod?
Can I be an angel?
Their parents came to watch, eyes fixed firmly on their own.
Lord, the stories abound.
Embryonic drama is enacted.
A good time is had by all.
There is a sixpence in the pudding.
The cake is cut.
The turkey is stripped bare.
And 'the Word became flesh'.
You become flesh in the enjoyment of children.
You become flesh in the forces that draw families together.
You become flesh in the selfish world of men, who force you to
    be born at the edge of a crowded inn.
Lord, become flesh within me.
I do not much mind whether there were angels and a manger,
    shepherds and eastern astrologers.
These stories form a cocoon around you.
Once you have burst forth, they no longer matter.
How many of those children, Lord, will ever see beyond the
    cocoon?
How many parents ever see beyond the superficialities surround-
    ing our lives?
Within this life of mine, within the years that lie ahead,
Lord, become flesh within me.

The Baptism of Jesus

Matthew 3.13-17

You identify yourself, Lord, with men who need the forgiveness of sins.
You submit to the baptism of John.
You are with us, you are for us.
You declare your interest.
You reveal at the beginning of your ministry the way you intend to go on.
You calm my fears that the dismal quality of my life might lead to the loss of your love.
Lord, identify yourself with my life.
In this is hope of improvement.

The Power Struggle

Matthew 4.1-11

Lord, I wrestle in the wilderness of temptation.
A force wells up inside: use your power for your own ends,
command these stones, throw yourself down, worship your-
self.
It is tempting, very tempting at times.
Those talents,
That influence,
That power,
You gave me them.
Talents, influence, power and the greatest of these is power.
I can use all three to boost my morale, to focus attention on
myself, to try and control my own destiny.
I can use all three in your service.
But it is not a simple matter of conflict, Lord, between love of
neighbour and love of self.
These are both inseparably intertwined.
A man calls.
I seek to help.
Is it because I too have stood where he is now standing?
Is it because of a feeling of guilt over a previous opportunity
missed?
Is it because others whose high regard I want to keep are watching
closely?
Is it because of the sense of inner satisfaction, fulfilment it brings?
Is it so as to feel justified in my own eyes?
Is it because we both are in need of your love?
I seek to help and find it hard to say why.
The motives are complex and hopelessly mixed.
But the struggle within, Lord, is not chiefly a struggle about
motives.
It is a struggle about freedom, independence, local government.
I want to be in full control, to do as I wish, to hide from myself
vast areas of experience that point to your presence.
I want my own way, Lord, even though it may coincide with yours.
I want control.

I want to be able to love my neighbour and feel that I am the
source of the love.
This is my struggle in the wilderness, Lord.
My desire for you has to fight its way through my desires to be
my own lord.
Whose is the power?
Is it mine alone, or yours?
You answer decisively: 'Do homage to the Lord your God and
worship him alone.'
Strengthen me in this power struggle.
This is my basic desire.

Little Peace for You, Lord

Mark 1.35-39

Little peace for you, Lord.
Little peace now that you have left the obscurity of Nazareth.
A brief quiet moment of prayer, but they sought you out.
You were back among people,
You were back to your mission.
Make me not to mind having my peace disturbed, Lord;
Only ensure that I have *some* peace that can be disturbed.

Transfiguration

Mark 9.2-8

Did Peter and James and John understand, Lord, then?
Do I understand now?
We all stand gaping.
We applaud because we feel we ought.
'How good it is that we are here!'
But do we understand?

A scruffy boy passed me in the street and suddenly flashed a
    smile.
A man spoke and turned an ordinary restaurant meal into a lively
    compelling occasion.
A woman listened and helped a man to maturity.
A power station with its monstrous cooling towers and elongated
    chimneys belching black smoke possessed a fascinating, in-
    dustrial beauty as it loomed out of an early morning mist.

Transfiguration happens daily, Lord.
But do I understand about yours?
Moses and Elijah, the law and the prophets, the symbols of all
    that went before, the symbols of previous experience, of past
    understanding, of accustomed habit, of usual ways, pale into
    insignificance when stood beside you.
They are set in perspective by your presence.
You are Lord.
Here I stand with my present relationships and experiences,
    opinions and beliefs, habits and conventions.
Here I stand with my gaze fixed firmly on you, Lord, if only for
    an instant.
Our encounter comes alive.
Your transfigured presence casts light over all that I am, and
    brings fresh meanings, new strength.
Transfigure, Lord, the whole of my life, the whole of all life.
Allow me to retain those meanings, that strength when the sense
    of your presence has gone.

Authority

Matthew 21.23-27

It would have been no good in any case, Lord, telling them that
    your authority was that of God.
You would only have incensed them more.
They would not have believed you.
Their minds were made up about you.
Their own authority was clear.
It was the authority of tradition, the authority of experience, the
    authority that springs from knowledge of the scriptures.
You had no authority.
You were a quack.
You had to be resisted, removed.
I feel some sympathy with them, Lord.
I have been trained as a priest.
I have some knowledge of the scriptures.
I have been ordained by the church.
I have been authorized like the Scribes and Pharisees.
How would the church survive without the knowledge, and in-
    sights, and wisdom handed down from the past?
How would it survive without the tradition of which I am part?
I feel some sympathy with them, Lord.
And yet I know you are right.
Your authority is the authority which matters.
You make a man decide for himself.
You make me responsible for the authority I let you have in my
    life.
You make me give or withhold authority.
Your words, your acts, your life, your death are gospel for me.
I am constrained to say that you speak with the power and chal-
    lenge of God.
Lord, I acknowledge your authority; help me acknowledge it.

It Had to be Shared

John 1.40-42

He was impressed, Lord.
He followed.
He saw.
He experienced.
His excitement could not be contained.
He could not keep it to himself.
It had to be shared.
He sought out his brother and brought him to you.
We have a need to share, Lord.
Life is too big to be possessed by one.
Love is not love until it is shared.
'No man is an island, entire of itself;
    every man is a piece of the continent, a part of the main.'
No man can be a man on his own; his humanity is shared.
It has to be shared.
A woman shares her life with her husband.
A child shares his joy with his parents.
A teacher shares his wisdom with a learner.
A husband shares his suffering with his wife.
Andrew knew his experience of you to be incomplete, Lord, until
    it could be shared.
You reach out to a man, and beyond him.
Your reach has no limits.
It stretches out to me, and yet leaves me behind unless I turn and
    follow its path to my neighbour.
Send me forth, Lord, as your apostle.

Consider the Signs

Matthew 11.2-10

John the Baptist sent his disciples to you, Lord, to enquire if you
were the Messiah, the expected one, the one around whom
all hopes were gathered.

He was not sure.

He wondered.

Perhaps he would turn in his grave to be likened to that young
man who planned to see a film with his girl.

They had agreed to meet at seven o'clock.

He was looking forward to it.

It was a good film and she was an attractive girl.

He felt proud to be seen with her.

He had not been going with her for long, but long enough to know
that he liked it and to think that she did too.

He reached the meeting point ten minutes early, but she was not
there yet.

They had said seven o'clock and she would probably be on the
next bus.

Time passed and she did not come.

Fifteen minutes, twenty minutes, half an hour and still there was
no sign of her.

He went over in his mind all the past signs of their relationship,
wondering if he had been deceiving himself, wondering if he
had misinterpreted the signs.

Or had she only been unavoidably delayed?

The Baptist too had been waiting, waiting for the Messiah.

He considered the signs; 'the blind recover their sight, the lame
walk, the lepers are clean, the deaf hear'.

But there are other, less happy, signs to consider; the innocent often
crushed by the guilty, greed achieving its goal, suspicion re-
placing truth, your challenging gospel swamped by inertia.

I am brought face to face with these signs, Lord, every day, both
good and bad.

I am brought face to face with them in the world, in others, in
myself.

I am brought face to face with them in your life too.

You are the one to bring sight to the blind, strength to the lame.
You are the innocent one crushed by the guilty.
The signs are all there, Lord.
Sometimes there are doubts, dissatisfactions, disasters,
But I opt for life.
Strengthen my decision.
Let my hopes and expectations in life gather around your presence,
    your risen and contemporary presence.
You are the 'one who is to come', and we have no need of another.

Which Way to Go?

Mark 2.1-12

'Your sins are forgiven. Arise and walk. Take up your bed and go.'
But where to, Lord?
No destination is mentioned.

' "Cheshire Puss", Alice began, "would you tell me please which
     way I ought to go from here?"
"That depends a good deal on where you want to get to", said the
     Cat.
"I do not much care where", said Alice.
"Then it does not matter which way you go", said the Cat.'

What happened to the man once sick of the palsy when he finally
     reached home with his bed on his back?
You forgave him, Lord.
You removed the invisible bonds that bound him to his bed.
You enabled him to carry away that which had held him captive.
What happened to him next?
Which way would he go?
You made him responsible for himself, Lord.
He was no longer to be carried, no longer someone else's re-
     sponsibility.
Which way would he go?
At the moment of his release there is joy, confidence, exhilaration
     at the new life he could now lead.
He was free!
Yet freedom has to be grasped, seized, taken to heart and con-
     tinually renewed.
Six months later are his sins weighing heavy on him again?
Is he back on his bed, with freedom of movement now, but no
     freedom to live?
Is he able to cope with his new freedom to choose?
There are dramatic moments of release, Lord, of forgiveness, of
     exaltation, moments when I am taken out of myself and
     touch eternity.
They determine the basis of life, the direction to go, the way
     ahead.

And you are that way, and your way leads to the cross.
Overcome my hesitations, my drawing back in anxiety.
Lead me in this way.
Let me take up my bed and follow.

People or Rules?

Mark 2.27-3.6

Saturday, Sunday, Monday, what difference does it make?
People are more important than rules.
A rule is a short cut to decision.
It saves time, energy;
It shows us where we stand.
But a rule raised to the level of Law becomes a god, an idol, a
    totem to be worshipped, come what may.
So the man carries his burden for longer than he need.
He comes seeking release, grace, love and many would have you
    turn him away.
You continually challenge all rules.
Lord, let me get my priorities right.
People are more important than rules.

'Who can This Be Whom even the Wind and the Sea Obey?'

Mark 4.35-41; Psalm 107.23-32

Your disciples included fishermen, Lord.
They were used to boats.
They knew about storms.
Here they take none of the usual precautions to keep the boat
    afloat in a storm.
It is odd.

'They cried to the Lord in their trouble, and he delivered them
    from their distress;
He made the storm be still, and the waves of the sea were hushed.'
'They were astonished and said to one another, "Who can this be
    whom even the wind and the sea obey?"'
My answer is ready, Lord.
You are God.
You can still the turbulent chaotic forces of life.
You can quieten the frightening raging of passion.
You can control the anxiety that wells up like a storm.
My answer is ready, Lord.
You are God.
'Then they were glad because they had quiet.
Let them thank the Lord for his steadfast love.'

Legion and those Pigs

Mark 5.1-20

'They begged Jesus to leave the district.'
Their economy would be ruined, if you made pigs behave like
    lemmings.
It is unusual.
It is peculiar.
It does not allow for convincing explanation.
It asks awkward questions.
We cannot get it taped, organized.
You threaten security.
We are quite happy looking after our pigs.
It is true that Legion is often to be heard shouting among the
    tombs.
But we keep away from there, especially after dark, and he does
    not trouble us.
Please go.
I am a little afraid of this power of yours.
It is too powerful.
You are master of one whom 'no one was strong enough to
    master'.
To commit myself totally to you, Lord, is a demanding thing
    to ask.
To be honest, there is part of my life I want to keep to myself.
There I can do as I please.
There I can be sole authority.
There I can be master.
There I can be lord.
To commit myself totally to you, Lord, would be to open to you
    the doors of this very private apartment.
I do not want you in, and yet I do.
It looks like being a life-long struggle, Lord, between that part of
    me that wants to control myself and the part that trusts to
    you.
Struggle with me, Lord.
And win.

A Last Resort for Jairus

Mark 5.21-24, 35-43

He was president of a synagogue.
He had probably been through all the procedures he knew to get
     his daughter well again.
He would come to you, Lord, as a last resort.
His pride as a leading member of the community is forgotten.
You might be preaching heresy.
You might be saying and doing all the wrong things.
Yet you seem to have power.
You might have the answer to his problem.
He came to you as a last resort.
There was no other hope.
His daughter is only twelve – as old as you were when, they say,
     you debated with the temple teachers.
You were on the threshold of life.
She is 'at death's door'.
You do not turn a man away, Lord, even when he comes only at
     the end of his tether.
On the contrary, then you are with him most of all.
As he gives of himself,
As he sacrifices his pride, his self-respect, his all,
As he throws himself down before you in faith,
Then you are with him most of all,
For then he is doing what you did on the cross,
Then he is becoming fully a man.
It takes courage, Lord.
Bring me to you in moments of strength as well as in moments
     of weakness.
Bring me to you.

Faith and Healing

Mark 5.25-34

She was a faithful believer.
Her sight had almost gone.
She went to a faith-healer, Lord.
There was no change in her condition,
Except that now there was a nagging doubt.
Perhaps she had not enough faith.
Perhaps it was her fault, or maybe you did not really care.
She read the story of the woman with the haemorrhage as a
    reproach.
Help her, and me, Lord, to see your healing power in the widest
    terms.
Our disabilities, disadvantages, weaknesses, troubles in life im-
    mediately come to mind.
We yearn for their removal.
And yet this is not always to be.
The real miracle of your healing power is the power of salvation,
    of wholeness, of reconciling a man with yourself.
It is the knowledge that the world has purpose, meaning, and that
    a man has a place in this, that I have a place in this.
'My daughter, your faith has cured you.'
Her faith and personal encounter with you, Lord, brought whole-
    ness, salvation and the cure was the seal of this.
Remove despair, self-reproach, anger when there is no cure, when
    we have to continue to live with our disabilities.
Strengthen us for this, by deepening our faith in you.

'Your Way was Through the Sea'

Mark 6.45-52; Psalm 77.16-19

I am tired, Lord,
Too tired to think,
Too tired to pray,
Too tired to do anything,
Too tired,
Drained of resources,
'Labouring at the oars against a head wind',
Pressed down by a force as strong as the sea.
Lord of all power and might,
'Your way was through the sea,
Your path through the great waters',
Calm my soul,
Take control,
Lord of all power and might.

Inner Loneliness

Mark 7.31-37

How great was his isolation, Lord.
Thank God he could see and smell and touch.
But he could not hear.
He could not speak.
He could not tell his spouse of his love.
He could not speak a word of sorrow but had to keep it bottled up within.
He could not communicate and share so many of the feelings and emotions and thoughts that welled up inside him.
He could not hear the joy of children.
He could not hear the word of comfort, consolation, encouragement that one man can pass to another.
He could not listen to the wisdom of others nor to the infectious laughter that raises the spirits.
Around his world was a barrier of silence.
Lord, you can break through all barriers.
You can enter our isolation and turn it into fellowship.
You work within the depths of my soul, the core of my personality, the heart of my inner self.
You are within.
You are without.
You are here.
Stay, Lord, and banish all isolation, inner loneliness.
Stay, Lord, and use me to banish the loneliness of others.

Blindness

Mark 8.17-26

Lord, you gave sight to the blind.
Your disciples were blind to the full meaning of your life.
They did not fully understand.
And who can blame them?
You had burst in on their lives.
You had attracted them.
You had got under their skins.
You had challenged them out of their rut.
You had found followers.
But they did not fully understand.
They only knew that this was what they must do, though the
    future was unclear.
Their eyes were gradually being opened, like the eyes of the man
    of Bethsaida.
They were beginning to see the truth that only dawned on them
    when you were dead, and risen.

My eyes see men that 'look like walking trees'.
My eyes see men and women enjoying themselves as life unfolds
    before them.
They see people in despair hanging on to life by their fingertips.
My eyes see many things that I only partly understand.

You have burst in on my life, Lord.
You have attracted me.
You have got under my skin.
You have challenged me out of my rut.
You have found a follower.
Help me to understand.
Open my eyes to see the way forward for myself, for the people
    among whom I live and work.
Open my eyes to see you.

Bartimaeus Makes a Scene

Mark 10.46-52

The people acted predictably, Lord.
They were embarrassed.
Bartimaeus was making a scene.
And we do not like scenes.
They make us uncomfortable.
They touch some force within us that cannot stand the pressure,
    and we strive to remove the offender.
That drunk who walked up to the bus queue and unleashed a
    torrent of obscenity.
'Call the police!'
'Get him away!'
'He ought to be locked up!'
That young man who spoke of his sin, his sense of guilt, un-
    worthiness.
A sudden hush descended as though we were in the eye of a
    hurricane.
That woman with the unconventional views refusing to obey the
    rules of cocktail superficialities.
Why, Lord, do we feel so uncomfortable?
Why?

You stopped.
Perhaps you were embarrassed.
I do not know.
But you stopped.
You saw Bartimaeus as a person.
You changed his life.
Lord, enable me to cope with the unconventional, the surprise,
    the irritating feelings of embarrassment.
Make me see persons, not patients, dropouts, clients,
                            not categories, classes, neatly parcelled ob-
    jects suitably labelled and controlled, but human persons.

If Only. . . .

John 5.1-9

I wonder if he really wanted to be cured, Lord.

For thirty-eight years he had been by the Sheep Pool, an old style Lourdes.

'I have no one to put me into the pool', he said, avoiding the question.

It is satisfying in a way, Lord, to indulge in a little self-pity.

It is satisfying in a way to justify this by having symptoms which provide the ideal excuse for not doing what has to be done.

It is satisfying in a way to stay as I am, in the ways I know, without taking the risks you urge on a man.

I see a little of myself in the lame Jew of Bethesda.

I see a little of myself in that story told of the rich hypochondriac who lived in a private hotel.

She bored her fellow residents with an incessant recital of her complaints.

It was as if she had studied all the diseases in the book.

'Work, work! How can I work? If only I were well, if only . . .'

When she hired a doctor as a professional private audience, he spoke the truth in love, but then 'he clearly did not understand!'

'Do you want to recover?' she was asked by a psychiatrist.

'No one has been able to help me. But if only . . .'

Perhaps, Lord, if she were well, her world would collapse around her, with no purpose to her life. She seemed unable to accept herself as a responsible person.

I see a little of myself, Lord, in all those people who are afraid of the responsibility of accepting themselves as they are, and of building on this.

If only I had had the education.

If only I had been born twenty years later.

If only I had a bit more money.

If only my job were more interesting.

Lord, you did nothing for the man by the Sheep Pool, except give him the urge to live.

He had to take to his feet and walk.

Lord, take away my excuses for refusing your life.

Give me the desire to live.

Give me the desire to take full responsibility for myself, and to be a man.

One among Five Thousand

John 6.1-14

What hope, Lord?
Shall I go? Shall I not?
How can I achieve anything among so many?
I am one among five thousand.
I feel like Philip: twenty pounds would not be enough to buy
bread to feed this crowd.
My resources doubled, trebled, quadrupled like those trading
stamps would still be insufficient.

I know in my heart that this is an excuse, Lord, that I am appre-
hensive of speaking out.
Whatever resources I have are your resources.
I am forgetting.
Two fishes and a handful of bread.
A cup of wine and a plate of bread.
What is that among so many?
It is strength, encouragement, challenge, salvation.
I offer you, Lord, my resources.
I offer you myself.
Recharge me with your power.
This is a real miracle.
Thank you, Lord.
I shall go.

The Easter Event

The passion narrative of St Mark, supplemented by stories from the other gospels, is the basis for the meditations in this concluding section. We begin with the entry into Jerusalem and pass through Gethsemane and the trials along the way to the cross, considering the influence of Jesus of Nazareth on the people involved in these events. We end with the resurrection – ascension happening. Although it is impossible to have any degree of certainty about what exactly happened on that first Easter morning, it is sufficient to know that something of vital significance did happen, which transformed our Lord's disciples from anxious and frightened individuals into a community of men encouraged and challenged to face whatever the future held for them, in the knowledge that the Jesus they had known and lived with was risen Lord, not only for them, but for the whole of the created order.

Into Jerusalem with Palms

Mark 11.1-10

It is an odd tale, Lord, full of symbolism, full of pointers to Old
Testament ideas.
It is an odd tale indeed.
Those secret passwords, an unridden colt, the pomp of palms.
You meant so much to your disciples.
You were the centre of their hopes, the focus of their aspirations.
They wanted to call you King.
And so do I, Lord.
But deliver me from blind obedience, unthinking response,
                from being immersed in a crowd that cheers or
    jeers without knowing why.
Crowds are frightening in the way they convert, cajole, pres-
    surize into agreement.
They throw palms and cheer.
They throw stones and shout crucify.
Make me think, Lord.
Make me use my mind.
Keep my eyes open across that leap of faith in you 'who come in
    the name of the Lord'.

Men of Power against Jesus

Mark 14.1-2

What a time to plan your death, Lord, the time of thanksgiving and joy for the release from Egypt!
The chief priests and elders are people with power.
They fight to preserve their status and authority, and seemingly do not much care what methods they use.
Of course it is better to do the job legally if possible, but a bribe here, some pressure there usually suffices.
They will be offended, Lord, if we were to say that they live by the law of the jungle.
They are found wherever power is.
They are found in all of us, Lord, in those attempts to keep at arms length whatever disturbs peace or threatens status.
They are found within that man whose only thought was to preserve his job.
They are found within our 'cunning plans' to use for our own comfort the wife, the child, the friend – the people who are bound to us by the intangible ties of relationship, and who are at the mercy of our power.
Lord, let us not use our power for our own ends.
Let me not exclude from my life the challenge of your person.
Let me not rationalize away the sharpness of your gospel.

'This is my body'

Mark 14.12-26

I am standing in a circle, Lord, among a few of your disciples in
   a small room.
I take a small piece of bread, a sip of wine.
This is your Body and Blood in which we all share.
I look around.
We all have our joys and sorrows, our hopes and disappointments.
We will go forth to love as best we can,
                     or to face some difficulty with renewed strength,
                     or to forget until we meet here again,
                     or to deny you with Peter,
                     or even perhaps to despair with Judas.
We, Lord, are your Body.
For the short time we meet together,
Draw us closer to yourself,
Make us aware of your presence,
Enable us to remove the sting from those problems that arise
   between us,
Weld us into that type of reconciled community you wish man-
   kind to be.
And then 'send us out in the power of your Spirit to live and work
   to your praise and glory'.

The Decision of Gethsemane

Mark 14.32-42

'Horror and dismay.'
There was no escape.
You were cornered.
Alone.
Your friends were asleep.
'Take this cup from me.'
You wanted release, as we all do, from the agony that stared you
    in the face.
Did you go over and over in your mind the events that led to
    Gethsemane?
Did you wonder if you had done the right thing?
Did you think that you may have made a mistake?
Did you feel the loneliness of rejection, by your friends, by God?
Doubt, anxiety, isolation, hell.
'Take this cup from me.'
'Yet not what I will, but what you will.'
No escape, but victory.
Strengthen my faith, Lord.
I have only two choices when faced with pain, suffering, Geth-
    semane.
Despair, cynicism, the meaninglessness of life.
Or 'Abba, Father. Your will be done.'
The logic of suffering demands of me a decision.
What do I say?
Is life 'yes' or 'no'?
Strengthen my faith, Lord.
Strengthen me to face the realities of life as you see it.
Strengthen me to share in your victory in Gethsemane.
'Abba, Father, your will, not mine, be done.'

Judas

Mark 14.10-11, 18-21, 43-46; Matthew 27.3-5

He could not live with himself.
His regrets were too great to be borne.
He committed suicide.
I find myself sympathizing with Judas, Lord.
Had he wanted to force your hand?
Had he heard you talk so much about God's Kingdom that he
    wanted some divine vindication?
Did he feel that by putting you on the spot God in you would
    be bound to act decisively, dramatically?
Perhaps he had even prayed about it and thought about it, only
    to see his whole scheme backfire in his face.
You were not able to produce the spectacular Judas may have
    wanted.
You just died – painfully.
And Judas was left to live with what he had done.
Only he could not.
Judas, Lord, is everyman in large letters.
He is everyman who has to live or die with his past.
The tragic irony of Judas, Lord, is that the cross and resurrection –
    the very things which he had helped to bring about – contain
    a gospel of hope that enables a man to pick himself up from
    the floor.
He impetuously took his life when forgiveness was so near.
Lord, strengthen those in despair.
Strengthen me to come to terms with myself and my actions in
    the light of your death and your resurrection.
'There is nothing in all creation that can separate us from the
    love of God in Christ Jesus our Lord.'

Peter's Problem

Mark 14.26-42, 66-72

He was an impetuous man, Lord,
As loyal to you as any of your disciples.
He would never dream of disowning his friendship.
A born leader,
A man of enthusiasm and zeal,
Worn out in Gethsemane,
Not really understanding the crisis that was upon you,
He slept.
When he awoke he saw you arrested, and was startled into those
   denials.

He, the firm follower, the rock, the man who had said that very
   day: 'Even if I must die with you, I will never disown you.'
Much later, they say, he was to die for you.
But then, at that moment of darkness, his sense of guilt was acute.
Little comfort to know that your eclipse, Lord, would have been
   total if your closest followers had all died with you.
The hardest thing would be for him to forgive himself, to regain
   some self-respect.
A lesser man might have let his guilt turn into a grudge against
   you.
He might not have been able to forgive you for causing his down-
   fall, and for standing as a constant reminder of what he had
   done.
Yet Peter's weakness, Lord, is a source of encouragement to your
   church.
He regained his balance.
He was able to accept your forgiveness and so forgive himself.
He stands as witness to the power of your forgiveness.
I confess my faith daily, Lord, and yet I disown you.
I have to draw near again and again to let your forgiveness sweep
   over me and allow me to forgive myself.
Thank you, Lord, for the life and witness of Peter.
His problem is my encouragement.

The Trial - an Excuse to Kill

Mark 14.55-64

You hardly spoke, Lord.
You said very little.
You did not defend yourself.
You offered no self-justifications.
This is impressive, Lord.
Especially so since you must have known that the trial was rigged,
    the case pre-judged.
They did not want to understand.
They were not interested in justice being seen to be carried out.
They were interested only in having an excuse to kill.
And yet you hardly spoke.
You made no attempt to convert them to your side.
You let your life and your personality speak for themselves.
And they did.
Only the court was not prepared to listen.
I wish I could follow your example, Lord.
It is so natural to want to be understood.
It is so natural to explain, to seek to justify what I do.
It is so natural to want critics to see my point of view.
How else will they realize that they have got it all wrong?
And yet you hardly spoke, Lord.
Your silence is impressive.
Your chief concern was not to justify yourself.
Raise my sights, Lord.

Who is Pilate?

Mark 15.1-15; John 18.28-19.16

Which one was Pilate, Lord?
Was he the common-sense man, the man with the answers,
the man trained and skilled in dealing with people,
the man able to keep both the people and Caiaphas happy,
the smooth skilled operator,
the capable competent man,
the successful man,
the man we all want to be?

Or was he the slightly uneasy man, the man who wonders,
the man whose easy veneer is disturbed by this enigmatic prophet
    Jesus,
the man who in spite of his background, responsibilities, training,
    still secretly, deep down, suspects that there may be more to
    this man who stands before him than meets the eye,
but a man who nevertheless is weak or cynical enough to say 'I
    find no case against him' as he gave Jesus up to be executed?
Why stir up trouble, a riot perhaps, for one perfectly expendable
    man?

Lord, help me to see beyond Pilate.
His soldiers had ensured that you were dead.
And his soldiers do not make mistakes.
All that you stood for was dead and buried.
And yet the tomb, they say, so carefully sealed and guarded, is
    empty.
Help me to see beyond Pilate.
To see beyond superficial ideals of success, competence, capability.
To see beyond those vague stirring doubts within that are never
    given a chance to emerge.
To see beyond values that are overvalued.
Give me faith in the new man condemned by the old.

The Luck of Barabbas

Mark 15.6-15

Barabbas must have laughed himself sick, Lord, that one of those
    odd quirks of history should secure his release.
What on earth could the crowd want with the release of a bandit?
A few strategically placed agents, loud passionate cries, and the
    crowd is alight, Jesus as good as dead.
Barabbas must have laughed at his luck.
I wonder if he reflected on how easily, how quickly we change
    our minds on matters that concern us only on the shallow
    level.
'Lord I believe, help my unbelief.'

The Passer-by from Cyrene

Mark 15.21

Was he afraid, Lord?
I expect so.
The soldiers bearing down on him, giving him no choice, forcing
him to carry the cross, that heavy cross.
Would they execute him too?
Was there fear in his heart as he walked along with Jesus to the
'place of a skull'?
To get involved in another man's problems carries risks and
anxieties with it.
Can I really be of help?
Can I listen?
Can I suffer along with the sufferer?
Do I have to feel, Lord, that I must be able to provide a pat
answer, a text-book solution?
Like the man from Cyrene, perhaps, my own security and com-
fort is at the front of my mind.
Support me, Lord, so that I may support that man over there who
has his cross to bear.

On the Cross

Mark 15.22-39

Proof.
We always want proof.
'Come down and we shall believe.'
Mankind was quite happy, thank you.
You only caused trouble.
Without proof there is nothing more to be said.
This was it.
The end.
The absolute end.

What could you see, Lord, as you looked down from the cross?
The women steeling themselves to watch from afar? And what
    did they think about it all?
The passers-by being as insensitive as the crowds that used to flock
    to Bedlam?
Your fellow-sufferers taunting you too? No doubt it took their
    minds off their own pain.
That man with a sponge, trying to be kind, shouting something
    about Elijah?
What could you see, Lord, as you looked down from the cross?

And that would have been that if certain things had not followed.
But how could you know then that there was more to follow?
'My God, my God, why have you forsaken me?'
It is impossible to penetrate the darkness that surrounds you.

Our inhumanity to each other is frightening, Lord.
You were made to stand where millions have also stood.
And we talk so glibly about involvement, incarnation.
Forgive us, Lord.
Words fail.

It is Accomplished!

John 19.30

The final word.
The new man is born.
Your purpose achieved,
You are man's freedom.
You have overcome the world.
You show the way,
You are the Way.
You are the centre of history, 'the divine milieu', the Alpha and
  Omega.
What more can be said?
You hang triumphant,
Lord,
In you I live and move and have my being.

Joseph the Councillor

Mark 15.1, 42-47

Was he, 'a respected member of the Council', a secret disciple,
  Lord?
Where was he when the chief priests 'with all the Council' con-
  demned you?
Did he concur with the cross?
Did he prudently keep out of the way?
You certainly had no friends in high places pulling strings.
Yet I cannot bring myself to censure him, Lord.
Would I have acted differently?
Perhaps it was his sense of shame that sent him to Pilate for your
  body.
But he took a risk and went.
He ensured a decent burial for your corpse.

Lord, let me not hide my faith in corners.
It is so very easy.
We secret disciples sit at home while you are eating with the
  despised.
We shake hands in the vestry while you are embracing the leper.
We enjoy the way things are while you are 'shaking the founda-
  tions'.
We talk in cliches while you challenge your listeners to decision.
We wear blinkers like those old-fashioned horses pulling those
  old-fashioned carts.
We get so used to them that we no longer realize that we only
  have half a view.
Remove, Lord, the anxieties and prejudices that obscure from me
  so much of your world and your will for this world.

Empty Tombs

Mark 16.1-8

Your tomb, they say, is empty.
Christ is risen, they say.
You are risen indeed, I reply.
Lord, deepen my faith in the new man 'born in a grave'.
Deepen my faith in myself to burst forth from the tomb within
　　that is so carefully sealed and guarded.
Deepen my faith, optimism, hope in life.
Deepen our faith in each other, so that we, the church, so care-
　　fully sealed and guarded against the Spirit may burst open with
　　new life.

Peace in the Room of Disappointments

John 20.19-29

The funeral party was over.
The crisis past.
You were dead.
Your disciples, Lord, met together behind locked doors.
That room is the place to which a man goes to cope with hopes
  that are unfulfilled.
That room is the room of disappointments.
And there they met.

But there too they were met, encountered by you, Lord.
You came alive in a group of disappointed men.
You brought peace and joy to their hearts.
You transformed them from disillusion to excitement.
You transformed them from a closed group behind locked doors to
  men prepared to live and speak openly as your followers.
No angels here, no pomp and pageantry.
Just an ordinary situation, ordinary men meeting together in
  sorrow.

Lord, come alive within my experience,
                within my sorrows and disappointments and
                    doubts,
                within the ordinary moments of my life.
Come alive as the peace and joy and assurance that is stronger
  than the locked doors within, with which we try to shut out
  life.
Come alive as the peace and joy and assurance that nothing in
  life or death can kill.

'It is True: the Lord has Risen'

Luke 24.13-35

Lord, I walk along the road to Emmaus.
My companion is the person I am with at any moment of time.
We communicate,
We talk,
We work,
We relax,
And for a while our crossed paths lead us together.
Sometimes between us there are invisible barriers which force
    us apart like two circles separated by the same tangent.
Sometimes the relationship is easy to make and grows in depth.
In our own ways and at varying levels we are striving for under-
    standing, meaning, some vision of a life that is worth leading.

And then the light dawns, and I know that you are there.
The new dimension to life is seen again.
It is one moment in a continual transformation, a moment of
    profound joy, the transfiguring of boredom and routine,
And it expands over all that I am.
Come, Lord,
And again I say:
'It is true: the Lord has risen.'

Resurrection

Matthew 28.16-20

I remember, Lord, the story Tolstoy tells of Prince Nekhludov,
A rich and opulent noble who had years before met a girl of
  fifteen and left her with a hundred rouble note and a child.
Their second meeting was traumatic for the Prince, now a judge.
She entered the courtroom, a prostitute, whose skin 'had the
  curious pallor that comes from long imprisonment, the sort
  of hue which brings to mind the shoots springing out from
  potatoes kept in a cellar'.
Nekhludov's mind was in a turmoil of fear, worry, guilt.
Yet out of the whirlpool of emotions came a gradual experience
  of rebirth, resurrection, as the gospel cast its light on his life.
'A new life began for him because everything that happened to
  him from that time held an entirely new and different meaning for him. Only the future will show how this new chapter
  of his life will end.'

It is a dramatic story, Lord.
Your disciples recognized an experience of a similar quality,
  'though some were doubtful'.
You took their past and challenged them to see it in a new light
  that remade their future.
You were with them always.
Your Spirit assured them, as it does me, of your eternal presence
  'to the end of time'.
Send us forth, Lord, in the power of your risen life.
Send us forth to live your resurrection.

You are more than Alive, You are Lord

Acts 1.1-11

You are not only risen and alive, you are Lord.
This is your ascension, your ascendancy over the whole universe.
You stand over and above all that is best in life as its source.
You stand above all that is worst as ultimate victor.
You stand above all powers and authorities as judge.
You stand above all failure and weakness and sin as forgiveness
    and love.
You alone are worthy of total allegiance, total commitment.
You are Lord,
'My Lord and my God.'

Appendix: A Brief Bibliography

G. B. Caird, *The Gospel of St Luke;* John Fenton, *The Gospel of St Matthew;* John Marsh, *The Gospel of St John;* D. E. Nineham, *The Gospel of St Mark:* Pelican Gospel Commentaries, Penguin Books.

T. G. A. Baker, *What is the New Testament?*, SCM Press 1969.

W. D. Davies, *The Sermon on the Mount*, CUP 1966.

C. H. Dodd, *The Parables of the Kingdom*, Collins Fontana Books 1961.

A. M. Ramsey, *The Narratives of the Passion*, A. R. Mowbray 1962.
The Resurrection of Christ, Collins Fontana Books 1960.

Index of Passages

The Easter Event